DATE DUE

OCT 0 2 2013			

HIGHSMITH 45230

The Emergence of Modern America

(1890-1930)

★★ PRESIDENTS OF THE UNITED STATES ★★

By Darlene Stille

WEIGL PUBLISHERS INC.

Published by Weigl Publishers Inc.
350 5th Avenue, Suite 3304 PMB 6G
New York, NY 10118-0069
Website: www.weigl.com

Library of Congress Cataloging-in-Publication Data

Stille, Darlene R.
  The emergence of modern America / Darlene Stille.
      p. cm. -- (Presidents of the United States)
  Includes bibliographical references and index.
  ISBN 978-1-59036-747-6 (hard cover : alk. paper) -- ISBN 978-1-59036-748-3 (soft cover : alk. paper)
  1. Presidents--United States--Biography--Juvenile literature. 2. Presidents--United States--History--20th century--Juvenile literature. 3. United States--History--1901-1953--Juvenile literature. 4. United States--Politics and government--1901-1953--Juvenile literature. I. Title.
  E176.1.S78 2008
  973.91092'2--dc22
                                2007012647

Printed in the United States of America
1 2 3 4 5 6 7 8 9 0 11 10 09 08 07

Project Coordinator
Heather C. Hudak

Design
Terry Paulhus

Photo Credits
Every reasonable effort has been made to trace ownership and to obtain permission to reprint copyright material. The publishers would be pleased to have any errors or omissions brought to their attention so that they may be corrected in subsequent printings.

All of the Internet URLs given in the book were valid at the time of publication. However, due to the dynamic nature of the Internet, some addresses may have changed, or sites may have ceased to exist since publication. While the author and publisher regret any inconvenience this may cause readers, no responsibility for any such changes can be accepted by either the author or the publisher.

Contents

United States Presidents

REVOLUTION AND THE NEW NATION (1750–EARLY 1800s)

 George Washington
(1789–1797)

 John Adams
(1797–1801)

 Thomas Jefferson
(1801–1809)

 James Madison
(1809–1817)

 James Monroe
(1817–1825)

EXPANSION AND REFORM (EARLY 1800s–1861)

 John Quincy Adams
(1825–1829)

 Andrew Jackson
(1829–1837)

 Martin Van Buren
(1837–1841)

 William Henry Harrison
(1841)

 John Tyler
(1841–1845)

 James Polk
(1845–1849)

 Zachary Taylor
(1849–1850)

 Millard Fillmore
(1850–1853)

 Franklin Pierce
(1853–1857)

 James Buchanan
(1857–1861)

CIVIL WAR AND RECONSTRUCTION (1850–1877)

 Abraham Lincoln
(1861–1865)

 Andrew Johnson
(1865–1869)

 Ulysses S. Grant
(1869–1877)

DEVELOPMENT OF THE INDUSTRIAL UNITED STATES (1870–1900)

 Rutherford B. Hayes
(1877–1881)

 James Garfield
(1881)

 Chester Arthur
(1881–1885)

 Grover Cleveland
(1885–1889)
(1893–1897)

 Benjamin Harrison
(1889–1893)

 William McKinley
(1897–1901)

THE EMERGENCE OF MODERN AMERICA (1890–1930)

 Theodore Roosevelt
(1901–1909)

 William H. Taft
(1909–1913)

 Woodrow Wilson
(1913–1921)

 Warren Harding
(1921–1923)

 Calvin Coolidge
(1923–1929)

THE GREAT DEPRESSION AND WORLD WAR II (1929–1945)

 Herbert Hoover
(1929–1933)

 Franklin D. Roosevelt
(1933–1945)

POST-WAR UNITED STATES (1945–EARLY 1970s)

 Harry S. Truman
(1945–1953)

 Dwight Eisenhower
(1953–1961)

 John F. Kennedy
(1961–1963)

 Lyndon Johnson
(1963–1969)

CONTEMPORARY UNITED STATES (1968 TO THE PRESENT)

 Richard Nixon
(1969–1974)

 Gerald Ford
(1974–1977)

 Jimmy Carter
(1977–1981)

 Ronald Reagan
(1981–1989)

 George H. W. Bush
(1989–1993)

 William J. Clinton
(1993–2001)

 George W. Bush
(2001–)

The Emergence of Modern America

People, trolleys, and carts made
State Street in Chicago, Illinois,
a busy place.

By the 1890s and early 1900s, the United States had serious social and political problems. These problems arose because of two great changes that took place after the Civil War. One change was the rapid growth of industry. Industries built factories, oil refineries, and steel mills in northern cities. The other change was the rapid growth of cities. Before the Civil War, only about six million people lived in U.S. cities. By 1910, that number had grown to 42 million. "**Progressives**," people with high ideals of fairness and democracy, wanted **reforms** to solve the problems caused by these changes. There were few controls on business in the late 1800s. Many industries were **trusts**. Trusts were monopolies controlled by one owner or one company. Trusts kept prices high and kept out competition. Factories could pay workers very low wages. Men, women, and children worked long hours in factories called "sweatshops."

At the same time, cities grew as people left farms to find jobs in the new industries. Some of the new city dwellers were **immigrants** from European countries. The rapid growth of cities led to the creation of slums. In New York City, for example, many thousands of people lived in filthy tenements, or buildings with many tiny apartments. Large families crowded into one or two rooms without heat or water. Some people had to live in slums because they could not earn enough money for a better life. Some people could not find jobs. Crime, poverty, and disease became major problems in slums.

In addition, some politicians took **bribes** from big businesses. These **corrupt** politicians used threats to make people vote for them. Some members of the police force were corrupt. People felt that they had lost their democratic form of government.

Progressive political leaders wanted to change these conditions. They broke up corrupt political machines. They sided with workers instead of industries. Progressives passed laws to control businesses and prevent child labor and long workdays.

Republican President Theodore Roosevelt and Democratic President Woodrow Wilson were both progressives. Republican presidents William Taft, Warren Harding, and Calvin Coolidge were **conservatives**. The conservatives feared that the progressives were making government too big. They wanted to give businesses more freedom to create wealth. Conservatives believed that this wealth would help everyone.

By 1920, most people were not interested in progressive reforms. They were more interested in buying automobiles, listening to the radio, and going to the movies. This carefree time in the United States came to an end when the stock market crashed in 1929. The next era, The Great **Depression**, began.

Theodore Roosevelt's Early Years

Theodore Roosevelt was born on October 27, 1858, in New York City. His father, also named Theodore, was a wealthy plate glass merchant. His mother's family owned a plantation in Georgia.

The Roosevelts were a very close family. "Teedie," as Theodore was called, had two sisters and one brother. The family took trips to see the wonders of the world. One year, they toured Europe. Another year, they traveled in Egypt.

> "It is hard to fail, but it is worse never to have tried to succeed."
>
> *Theodore Roosevelt*

When the Civil War broke out in 1861, Theodore's father supported the North. His mother sympathized with the South, or the Confederacy. Most northerners believed that slavery was wrong. Some people in the South owned slaves and relied on them to work their plantations. Nevertheless, Theodore's parents never let their views about the Civil War cause any problems in their household.

Young Theodore's childhood was ideal, except for his asthma. The disease made him weak and sick. Theodore discovered that he could not see as well as other children. He was nearsighted and had to wear glasses. When Theodore became a teenager, his father encouraged him to build up his body. Theodore began to exercise in a home gym. Over time, he became strong and healthy.

Theodore Roosevelt became the 26th president of the United States.

Theodore attended Harvard University and graduated in 1880. That same year, he married Alice Lee. Theodore's father died and left him some money, but it was not enough to live on. After graduating, Theodore had to earn a living. He tried law school, but thought it was boring. Finally, he decided on a career in politics.

In 1881, Roosevelt was elected to the New York state assembly. He soon became a Republican leader in the assembly. Roosevelt had a bright political future until tragedy struck.

On the same day in 1884, he lost both his mother and his wife. Roosevelt's mother, Martha, died of typhoid. Alice died after giving birth to a daughter. Roosevelt named the baby Alice. He was so saddened that he left baby Alice with his sister and headed out to the badlands of the Dakota Territory. He became a cattle rancher and lived the strenuous life of a cowboy.

After two years of ranch life, most of Roosevelt's cattle had died because of severe winter storms. He decided to return to New York. In 1886, Roosevelt married a childhood friend, Edith Carow. He built a home called Sagamore Hill on Long Island. There, the couple began raising five children of their own and Roosevelt's daughter Alice.

Roosevelt had one daughter, Alice, with his first wife. Theodore, Kermit, Ethel, and Archibald were four of the five children he had with his second wife, Edith.

Roosevelt's Early Political Career

Roosevelt decided to try politics again. In 1886, he lost an election for mayor of New York City but was appointed to the U.S. Civil Service Commission in 1889. He helped set up civil service exams for jobs. In 1895, he became commissioner of the New York City Police Department and worked to rid the city of police officers who accepted bribes or neglected their duties.

Roosevelt believed that a powerful nation had to have a strong navy. In 1897, he became assistant secretary of the navy and worked to build more U.S. ships. At the time, Spain ruled Cuba. The Cubans wanted independence from Spain. Roosevelt thought the United States should go to war with Spain to help Cuba in its quest.

> "I have always been fond of the West African proverb, 'Speak softly and carry a big stick, and you will go far'."
>
> *Theodore Roosevelt*

The battleship U.S.S. *Maine* was in Havana Harbor when it exploded and sank in February 1898. The cause of the explosion was never discovered, but many people believed that Spain was responsible. These suspicions helped start the Spanish-American War in April 1898.

The U.S.S. *Maine* entered Havana Harbor in January 1898. An explosion sunk the ship in February of that year, triggering the Spanish-American War.

Roosevelt organized a group of volunteers to fight in the Spanish-American War.

Roosevelt put together a group of volunteer cavalry called the Rough Riders. He led them in a well-known charge in the Battle of San Juan Hill in Cuba. Roosevelt became a national hero. Spain surrendered in July and not only left Cuba but gave Puerto Rico, Guam, and the Philippines to the United States.

After the war, Roosevelt was elected governor of New York state. He disliked officials who took bribes and gave government jobs to friends. Roosevelt believed in honesty, fair play, and hard work. He began to reform the state government. He signed a law taxing businesses. Some Republican leaders thought Roosevelt was doing too much too quickly.

Roosevelt was elected vice president when President William McKinley won re-election in 1900. McKinley, however, was assassinated in September 1901. At age 42, Roosevelt became the youngest president of the United States.

As president, Roosevelt advocated reform. He warned about the power of railroads. Railroads were controlled by trusts that set prices and drove away competition. Roosevelt enforced the Sherman Antitrust Act. It was passed in 1890 to control the monopolies. Through the act, Roosevelt was able to break up railroad and oil trusts. He became known as a "trust buster."

THE TEDDY BEAR

President Roosevelt went on a bear hunt with some guides. After several days, they were unable to find a bear. Finally, one of the guides found an old bear. He let his dogs at the bear, and they injured it. The guides tied the bear to a tree so President Roosevelt could shoot it. Roosevelt refused to shoot the old bear for sport.

This quickly became a popular story, and a political cartoonist drew a cartoon showing "Teddy" Roosevelt refusing to shoot a cute little bear.

A shopkeeper by the name of Morris Michtom saw the cartoon. His wife had made some stuffed bears, and the cartoon gave him an idea. He asked Roosevelt if he could call the stuffed bears, "Teddy Bears." Roosevelt agreed, and the teddy bear was born.

The Square Deal

When Theodore Roosevelt became president, industries such as coal mining and steel making had become large and powerful. Their owners became rich. The workers in these industries, however, worked long hours and were paid very little. Often the places where they worked were dirty and dangerous. To increase their chances of bargaining with big companies, they formed **unions** that would represent their best interests. The coal miners formed a union called the United Mine Workers.

In 1902, coal miners in Pennsylvania went on **strike**. The miners had asked the mine owners for a pay increase and an eight-hour workday. They wanted the mine owners to recognize the United Mine Workers Union. The owners refused all of these demands. The miners refused to come to work until the owners met their demands.

Most people in the United States sympathized with the miners. The strike went on for months. People began to worry about where they would get coal for the coming winter. Coal was used to heat homes, stores, hospitals, and schools. Industries needed coal to operate factories and steel mills.

Coal miners in Pennsylvania went on strike for better wages and shorter workdays.

President Roosevelt decided to help settle the strike. He invited the miners and mine owners to meet at the White House. He asked both sides to let an outside group of experts decide how the strike should be settled.

Roosevelt wanted to help the miners. No president had ever tried to settle a labor **dispute** by taking the side of the workers. He threatened to take over the mines and send federal troops to mine the coal. This concerned the mine owners, and they agreed to settle the strike. The workers won a 10 percent wage increase and shorter working hours.

A "square deal" is what Roosevelt said he was seeking for the workers. He believed that factory and mine owners had too much power. Roosevelt asked Congress to create the Department of Labor and Commerce, which they did in 1903. He called for Congress to pass laws that would **regulate** industries to protect workers and consumers. Roosevelt worked to make the square deal for business and labor a part of life. The square deal became his campaign slogan for the 1904 election.

"We demand that big business give the people a square deal; in return we must insist that when anyone engaged in big business honestly endeavors to do right he shall himself be given a square deal."

Theodore Roosevelt

Many working-class people supported Theodore Roosevelt.

Roosevelt's Second Term

Roosevelt campaigned in 1904 for another term as president. He won the election by a landslide. The president continued trying to control the powerful railroads. Railroads gave **rebates** to big businesses that shipped large amounts of goods. This meant that the businesses received money back on their shipping costs. As a result, big companies paid less to ship goods than smaller ones. This practice did not fit in with Roosevelt's philosophy of fair play. In 1903, Congress passed the Elkins Act, making rebates illegal. At Roosevelt's request, Congress passed the Hepburn Act of 1906, allowing the federal government to change shipping rates that it considered unfair.

> "The conservation of natural resources is the fundamental problem. Unless we solve that problem it will avail us little to solve all others."
>
> *Theodore Roosevelt*

Some of the things Roosevelt did were based on his interest in nature and wildlife. He believed in preserving the environment and wilderness areas. In 1905, he set up the U.S. Forest Service. During his presidency, he doubled the number of national parks from five to ten and set up the first protected areas for birds and game. He also established 18 national monuments, including the Grand Canyon.

Roosevelt became concerned about food and medications. In 1906, he read *The Jungle*, a novel by Upton Sinclair about **unsanitary** practices in meat packing plants. Roosevelt persuaded Congress to pass pure food and medication laws. These laws regulated the quality of food and medication.

Roosevelt made the Grand Canyon a national monument in 1908. It became Grand Canyon National Park in 1919.

When European countries threatened military action against Latin American countries who did not repay their loans, Roosevelt enforced and extended the Monroe Doctrine of President James Monroe. The doctrine forbade any European power from interfering with any nation in the Western Hemisphere. Roosevelt added what became known as the Roosevelt **Corollary** to the Monroe Doctrine. In this corollary, Roosevelt stated that the United States could intervene in Latin America if necessary.

Roosevelt became known as a peacemaker. He helped settle disputes between other nations. He helped end a war between Japan and Russia by negotiating their commercial rights in China. For his efforts, he won the Nobel Peace Prize. Hearing of his mediation skills, the German Kaiser asked Roosevelt to help settle a dispute involving Germany, France, and Great Britain. The three countries were fighting over commercial rights in Morocco. Roosevelt feared that Europe would go to war over the issue. He was able to help the countries come to an agreement.

Although he was a peacemaker, Roosevelt believed his country should be ready for war. He persuaded Congress to build up the army and the navy. He sent 16 battleships and other warships of the Atlantic fleet to visit countries from 1907 to 1909. The ships were painted white, and they became known as the Great White Fleet. The Great White Fleet was a show of strength. It let other countries

know what they would face if they started a war with the United States.

The Nobel Peace Prize was awarded to Roosevelt in 1906.

PANAMA CANAL

Roosevelt decided to build a canal through Panama to connect the Atlantic and Pacific Oceans. He believed that U.S. warships should be able to move quickly from one ocean to another. France had already attempted to build a canal in Panama. At that time, Panama was part of Colombia. Colombia would not allow the French to build the canal. Roosevelt helped Panama become independent in 1903, and Panama and the United States then signed a treaty. In 1906, Roosevelt visited Panama to see the canal's progress. He was the first president to visit a foreign country while in office.

Roosevelt's Achievements and Legacy

Theodore Roosevelt saw himself as the president of the people. He believed in fair play and put his ideas into action. He broke up more than 40 powerful trusts. Roosevelt was not against business, but he believed that businesses should profit by fair competition. He urged Congress to pass laws that protected consumers, workers, and owners of small businesses.

Roosevelt helped make the United States a world power. He believed that having a strong military was important. Roosevelt used his military to uphold and strengthen the Monroe Doctrine, keeping European forces out of the Western Hemisphere.

Theodore Roosevelt served as president from 1901 to 1909.

While he was president, Roosevelt feared that war might break out among nations in Europe. By helping them to solve their differences, historians believe that Roosevelt delayed the start of World War I.

Some of Roosevelt's greatest achievements were in conservation. He protected more than 230 million acres of wilderness from logging and mining. He set up wildlife preserves, national forests, and national parks.

When World War I broke out in Europe in 1914, President Wilson at first refused to send U.S. troops. Roosevelt criticized Wilson for not declaring war on Germany. When the United States entered the war in 1917, all four of Roosevelt's sons served. His daughter, Edith, served as a nurse in the war. One of Roosevelt's sons was killed in the war in July 1918.

Six months after the death of his son, Roosevelt died in his sleep. His death came as a surprise. The nation mourned the loss of their former president.

Many historians believe that Roosevelt created the modern presidency. Roosevelt believed that the president should have great power. He shifted power from Congress to the president, and the president became the center of U.S. politics. The presidents who served after Roosevelt had more power than the presidents who served before him.

In 1947, Theodore Roosevelt Memorial Park, which includes his cattle ranch, was established in North Dakota. The park stands as a memorial to his contribution to conservation and the environment. It became a national park in 1978.

People enjoy recreational activities, such as horseback riding, in Theodore Roosevelt National Park.

> "I do not believe that any president ever had as thoroughly good a time as I have had, or has ever enjoyed himself as much."
>
> *Theodore Roosevelt*

THE BULL MOOSE PARTY

Roosevelt wanted William Taft to be the next president. The Republican Party was divided. Progressive Republicans supported Roosevelt's reforms. Conservative Republicans did not. Taft promised to continue Roosevelt's progressive policies, and he was elected in 1908.

Roosevelt went hunting in Africa. When he returned, he found that Taft had become more conservative. Roosevelt decided to run for president again in 1912. He helped form the Progressive Party, nicknamed the "Bull Moose" Party. Roosevelt was asked if he thought he was healthy enough for another four years in office. He replied that he was as fit as a bull moose, giving his party the nickname. Roosevelt called for giving women the right to vote, providing unemployment insurance, and setting up pensions for senior citizens. The division of the Republican Party allowed Democrat Woodrow Wilson to win the election. After his defeat, Roosevelt urged the Progressive Party to again join with the Republican Party.

William Taft's Early Years and Early Political Career

William Howard Taft was born on September 15, 1857, in Cincinnati, Ohio, to Alphonso and Louisa Torrey Taft. The Taft family grew to include five boys and one girl. Two of William's brothers had been born to his father's first wife, who died in 1852.

The Taft family was wealthy and well established. Alphonso was a lawyer and judge. He was a very important person in the Republican Party. He had served as secretary of war and attorney general under President Ulysses S. Grant. Louisa was an independent, energetic woman who spent much of her time advocating for programs in education and the arts.

William Taft was the 27th president of the United States.

William was a happy, good-natured boy. He enjoyed playing baseball, swimming, and skating. Taft did well in school. He attended Yale University and graduated in 1878. He then studied law and received his degree from the University of Cincinnati Law School in 1880.

Taft enjoyed law. He especially liked being a judge. He was appointed and then elected judge of the Cincinnati Superior Court, solicitor general of the United States, and judge of the federal circuit court. His dream was to be a justice of the U.S. Supreme Court, the highest court in the land.

> "Don't sit up nights thinking about making me President for that will never come and I have no ambition in that direction. Any party which would nominate me would make a great mistake." *William Taft*

Taft's wife had other ideas. He had met Helen Herron at a sledding party, and they were married in 1886. The couple had three children. Helen Taft wanted her husband to be president of the United States, not just a judge. She urged Taft to enter national politics.

In 1901, President William McKinley, a Republican, appointed Taft governor of the Philippine Islands. Spain, after losing the Spanish-American War, had turned the Philippines over to the United States. Taft moved his family to the Philippines and helped the country establish a new government. Taft enjoyed the Philippines, and the Filipino people supported him.

In 1904, Taft was appointed secretary of war under President Roosevelt. This position allowed Taft to stay involved in the Philippines. Taft and Roosevelt became good friends. Roosevelt sent Taft all over the world to deal with foreign affairs. Roosevelt appointed Taft and his war department to oversee the building of the Panama Canal.

Taft and his wife, Helen, had two sons and a daughter.

Taft's Presidency

Theodore Roosevelt had vowed that he would not run again after his second term ended in 1909. Instead, Roosevelt and other progressives believed that Taft would continue Roosevelt's reforms. The reforms included Roosevelt's square deal and breaking up trusts.

At this time, the Republican Party was divided between progressives and conservatives. The progressives favored social reforms and controls on railroads and industries. The conservatives preferred to leave businesses alone.

Roosevelt asked Taft to be the Republican presidential candidate. At first, Taft refused. He wanted to be appointed to the Supreme Court, not run the country. Roosevelt and Taft's wife talked him into running. At the Republican National **Convention**, Taft won the nomination on the first ballot.

Taft attended baseball games in New York.

In the election, Taft beat his Democratic opponent by more than a million votes. He was sworn in as president in March 1909. Taft did not look forward to being president. He knew that he was nothing like Roosevelt. "There is no use trying to be William Howard Taft with Roosevelt's ways," Taft said. "Our ways are different."

Just how different their ways were soon became clear. The party remained split between progressives and conservatives. Taft tried to continue the progressive policies, but he soon angered the progressives. He did not appoint any progressives to his Cabinet. Then, he supported the Payne-Aldrich **Tariff**. Progressives in the Republican Party wanted U.S. tariffs lowered. Taft called on Congress to pass a bill lowering Tariffs. Instead, Congress passed the Payne-Aldrich Tariff. This bill lowered some tariffs but kept most tariffs high. The progressives wanted Taft to veto the bill. Instead, he signed it into law.

A problem involving conservation ended progressive support for Taft in 1909. Roosevelt and the progressives believed it was very important to protect the nation's natural resources. The chief forester accused the secretary of the interior of acting against Roosevelt's conservation policies. The chief forester said the interior secretary had sold land to companies too cheaply, sometimes breaking the law. Taft supported the interior secretary and fired the chief forester. Progressives were angry and turned against Taft.

> **"I am afraid I am a constant disappointment to my party."**
> *William Taft*

Taft did not want to be president, but he ran in the 1908 election and won.

The Election of 1912 and Taft's Legacy

In 1910, Roosevelt returned from a hunting trip in Africa. Progressives urged him to run for president again. At first, Roosevelt refused. Taft continued to side with the Conservatives, however, and the two men became bitter enemies. In the end, Roosevelt tried for the Republican Party nomination in 1912.

Taft and Roosevelt faced each other in the Republican primary elections. The Conservatives backed Taft, and the Progressives backed Roosevelt. Republican voters clearly wanted Roosevelt as the party's candidate.

Although Roosevelt won most of the primary elections, Taft and the Conservatives controlled the Republican National Convention. They made sure that most of the convention **delegates** voted to nominate Taft. The Progressives accused the Conservatives of "stealing" the nomination. Roosevelt and the progressives formed a new party, the Progressive Party. The Progressive Party nominated Roosevelt as its candidate.

Taft had no doubt that he would lose the election because of the split in the Republican Party. In the general election, Taft was defeated. The Democratic candidate, Woodrow Wilson, received the most votes. Roosevelt came in second.

> "I'm glad to be going. This is the lonesomest place in the world."
>
> *William Taft said of leaving the White House*

Theodore Roosevelt (left) chose William Taft (right) to succeed him as president, but the two became rivals when they ran against each other in the 1912 election.

Taft made a number of reforms while he was president. He was a greater "trust buster" than Roosevelt. Taft broke up about 90 trusts, while Roosevelt broke up about 40. Taft asked the heads of federal bureaus to report on the money they needed. This step led to the setting up of a federal budget.

He urged Congress to pass a number of measures that had far-reaching effects. Congress expanded the powers of the Interstate Commerce Commission, which regulated the economics of railroads, trucking companies, and other transportation industries. Congress also passed a law that required candidates in federal elections to reveal how much they spent on their campaigns. During Taft's presidency, the 16th amendment to the Constitution was passed. This amendment called for a federal income tax.

First Lady Helen Taft made a lasting contribution to Washington, D.C. When the Tafts lived in the Philippines, Helen loved the blossoming cherry trees she saw there. As First Lady, she encouraged the emperor of Japan to donate 3,000 cherry trees to the people of the United States. Every spring, visitors to the capital can see pink and white cherry blossoms around the Tidal Basin.

Taft left the White House in March 1913. He became a professor of constitutional law at Yale University. He was elected president of the American Bar Association. During World War I, President Wilson appointed Taft to the National War Labor Board, which settled problems between businesses and labor. Wilson then put Taft in charge of the League to Enforce Peace, which worked for a league of nations, a world court, and mandatory international conciliation.

The Tafts left a lasting legacy in Washington, D.C.

Taft and the Supreme Court

Taft's long-time dream came true in 1921. Republican Warren Harding had just been sworn in as president. The post of chief justice was available on the U.S. Supreme Court. President Harding appointed Taft to the post.

This was a great honor. The Supreme Court's job is to uphold the Constitution as the supreme law of the United States.

The judges on the Supreme Court are called justices. Congress sets the number of justices. The president appoints the justices with the "advice and consent" of the Senate. This means that the Senate votes to approve a justice. Today, as when Taft served, there are eight associate justices and one chief justice.

> "Presidents come and go, but the Supreme Court goes on forever."
> *William Taft*

The justices rule on whether actions by federal, state, or local governments are constitutional. They make rulings based on laws passed by Congress and on treaties with other nations. They rule on whether decisions by lower federal or state courts are called for by the Constitution. They rule on court cases about disagreements between states.

Taft realized his dream of becoming a Supreme Court justice in 1921.

The justices might not all agree about a case, so they take a vote. At least five justices must agree about a Supreme Court ruling for it to pass.

The Supreme Court justices hear very few cases. They only pick the most important cases that will help other judges and lawyers make decisions in future trials. Lawyers from each side argue a case before the justices.

When Taft took over as chief justice, the Supreme Court was far behind in its work. Taft set about organizing the Supreme Court's work. He asked Congress to pass the Judge's Act of 1925, a law that allows Supreme Court justices to decide which cases they will hear.

One of Taft's most important decisions had to do with the power of the president. Taft ruled that the Constitution gives the president the power to fire high-level federal employees, such as a postmaster. He and other justices ruled that courts could not stop workers from organizing a union or going on strike.

By 1930, Taft had serious heart trouble. He retired from the court in February. He died on March 8. Taft was buried in Arlington National Cemetery in Virginia. John F. Kennedy is the only other president buried there.

On November 8, 1930, a delegation of boy scouts honored Taft at his grave site in Arlington National Cemetery.

Woodrow Wilson's Early Years

Thomas Woodrow Wilson was born in Staunton, Virginia, at the end of December 1856. The Wilson family records are not clear about his actual birth date. Thomas was one of four children born to Joseph Wilson and Janet Woodrow Wilson. As a boy, his friends and family called him Tommy. When he grew up, he wanted to be called Woodrow, so he dropped his first name.

When Wilson was growing up, great Civil War battles were being fought in the South. He saw the kind of hardships that war causes. His father, a Presbyterian minister, turned his church into a hospital for wounded Confederate soldiers.

Most schools in the South were closed during the Civil War. Wilson was not able to attend school until he was nine years old. Wilson's parents valued education and taught him his lessons at home. Wilson's father took him on trips to see new things. They visited iron foundries and factories where ammunition was made. Afterward, Wilson and his father discussed what they had seen.

When Wilson was 16 years old, he enrolled at Davidson College in North Carolina. The school still had problems caused by the war. Wilson and the other students had to do chores, such as carrying in water and wood for fires.

In 1875, Wilson entered the College of New Jersey, now called Princeton University. He was an excellent student and enjoyed debating. After graduating, he went to Virginia Law School in Charlottesville, Virginia.

Woodrow Wilson was the 28th president of the United States.

Wilson and his first wife, Ellen, were married for nearly 30 years before she died in 1914.

Wilson was a lawyer for a short time. He decided he would rather teach college. He studied history and political science at Johns Hopkins University. He earned a Ph.D. degree in 1886.

While a student, Wilson married Ellen Louise Axson in 1885. The couple had three children. Wilson greatly enjoyed his children. He told them stories and played games with them.

Wilson taught at Princeton University and other schools. In 1902, he became president of Princeton. Wilson tried to make changes. He wanted students to focus more on learning and less on social events. Not everyone liked his ideas. Newspapers printed stories about the changes Wilson wanted to make. The stories showed Wilson as a person who cared more for working-class people than for the wealthy.

> **"...people call me an idealist. Well, that is the way I know I am an American. America is the only idealistic nation in the world."**
> *Woodrow Wilson*

Wilson's Presidency

Leaders of the Democratic Party in New Jersey watched Wilson's career. They were impressed with his honesty and leadership abilities. They convinced Wilson to run for governor, and he won the election of 1910. He then worked for honesty in state government, better education for students, and other progressive reforms. When the legislature would not pass one of his reforms, he went to the people. He made public speeches telling why reform was needed.

> "We can afford to exercise the self-restraint of a really great nation which realizes its own strength and scorns to misuse it."
>
> *Woodrow Wilson*

As governor, Wilson was very popular. He became well known across the nation. In 1912, he decided to run for president. He was nominated by the Democratic Party and won. He might not have won, however, if there had not been a split in the Republican Party. With the Republican vote split, Wilson became the first president born in the South to be elected since the Civil War.

Wilson took office on March 4, 1913. He asked Congress to pass a number of reforms. The first was lowering or removing most tariffs, a tax the government places on imported goods. The second was to set up a central banking system under the control of a Federal Reserve Board. The Fed, as it became known, oversees banking, interest rates on loans, and the money supply. Wilson had Congress pass laws to regulate industries, set up an eight-hour workday in the railroad industry, and prohibit child labor.

Wilson's presidency was full of issues involving foreign nations. In Mexico, in

Wilson was elected governor of New Jersey in 1910.

A German submarine attacked the *Lusitania*, an ocean liner that was carrying civilians. About 1,200 people died in the attack and its aftermath.

1913, Victoriano Huerta, a Mexican general, overthrew the Mexican government and declared himself dictator. Wilson refused to recognize Huerta and tried to negotiate peace between Huerta and the former government. Neither side agreed to negotiate. Unwilling to go to war, Wilson asked some Latin American countries to intervene, and Huerta fled Mexico. Another situation arose in 1916, when a Mexican rebel leader named Pancho Villa raided a town in New Mexico. Nineteen Americans were killed in the raid. Wilson sent troops into Mexico to chase Villa. For the second time in three years, the United States and Mexico almost went to war.

The greatest foreign concern, however, was in Europe. World War I broke out in 1914. The Allies, headed by Great Britain, France, and Russia, went to war against the Central Powers, headed by Germany and Austria-Hungary. Wilson declared that the United States would stay neutral. It would not support either side in the war. Wilson stayed neutral even after a German submarine sank the British ocean liner *Lusitania*. About 1,200 people died, including 128 Americans.

In 1914, tragedy struck Wilson's personal life. His wife died of kidney failure after an illness. In 1915, he met a widow named Edith Bolling Galt. They married in December of that year.

World War I

World War I, or the Great War as it was then called, caused more destruction and killed more people than any war up to that time. Before the war, there were empires in central Europe. They were controlled by royal rulers. An empire called Austria-Hungary was made up of Austria, Hungary, Bosnia-Herzegovina, and a number of other small countries. Austria-Hungary contained many groups of people with different languages and cultures. One royal family ruled Austria-Hungary. Russia had a royal ruler called a czar. Germany had a ruler called the kaiser. What is now Turkey was called the Ottoman Empire. It was ruled by a sultan.

Germany had built up powerful armed forces. Other European countries feared Germany's power. France, Russia, and Great Britain formed an alliance. They promised to go to war if a country in the alliance was attacked.

> "There must be, not a balance of power but a community of power; not organized rivalries but an organized, common peace.
>
> *Woodrow Wilson*

This map's color key shows the alliances of European countries in 1914, at the start of World War I.

Historians still debate the causes of World War I. The events that set off the war began with an assassination. A Serbian student shot Austrian Archduke Ferdinand in Bosnia-Herzegovina. Austria-Hungary blamed Serbia, a neighboring county, for the attack. Austria-Hungary declared war on Serbia. France, Russia, and Great Britain took Serbia's side. Germany and the Ottoman Empire sided with Austria-Hungary. Soon, all the countries of Europe were fighting. Countries that sided with Germany and Austria-Hungary were called the Central Powers. Countries that sided with France, Russia, and Great Britain were called the Allies.

An **armistice**, an agreement to stop fighting, ended the war in 1918. By then, about nine million soldiers on both sides had been killed, and about 21 million others wounded. Towns, farms, railroads, and bridges in Belgium and France were completely destroyed. The royal rulers of Germany, Russia, and Austria-Hungary were overthrown.

The Allies met in Paris to draw up a peace settlement. Wilson presented what were called the Fourteen Points for a fair treaty and a lasting peace. The Fourteen Points was a plan for ending World War I and setting up an association of nations. These points included freedom of the seas, equal free trade, weapons reduction, and more.

The European Allies paid no attention to most of Wilson's ideas. They wanted

World leaders gathered in Paris, France, to sign a treaty to end World War I.

to punish the Central Powers. They especially wanted to punish Germany. The Allies prepared peace agreements for each of the Central Powers. The treaty with Germany was called the Treaty of Versailles. The treaty took away land from Germany. The land became part of Belgium, Czechoslovakia, Denmark, France, and Poland. The Allies demanded that Germany make huge payments to cover the war damages. This treaty set the foundation for World War II.

The United States Enters World War I

Wilson ran for re-election in 1916 and won. His campaign slogan was, "He kept us out of war." After Wilson began his second term, things changed quickly. German submarines attacked U.S. ships. The British government found proof that Germany was plotting to start a war between Mexico and the United States. In April 1917, Wilson asked Congress to declare war against Germany to make the world "safe for democracy." The United States entered World War I on the side of the Allies.

Wilson urged everyone to support the war effort. Factories made uniforms, boots, guns, and other items needed for war. The government drafted men to become soldiers. Women volunteered to be nurses and clerks. About two million U.S. troops went to Europe. They helped the Allies win great battles in France and Belgium.

> **"The world must be made safe for democracy. Its peace must be planted upon the tested foundations of political liberty."**
>
> *Woodrow Wilson*

The British welcomed U.S. soldiers as they marched through the streets of London.

In January 1918, Wilson delivered an important speech to Congress. It contained his Fourteen Points for lasting peace. On Nov. 11, 1918, the nations at war signed an armistice.

In Paris, the Allies drew up the Treaty of Versailles, ending the war and calling for the League of Nations. Wilson worked hard to get the U.S. Senate to ratify, or approve, the treaty. Many senators did not want the United States tangled up with Europe. They would not ratify the treaty.

Wilson set off on a U.S. tour to tell citizens about the treaty. He wanted the people of the United States to support his idea for a League of Nations. Wilson had been working very hard. He was tired, and his health suffered. He had a stroke in October 1919 that paralyzed him on one side. His wife, Edith, tried to keep his illness a secret. She kept visitors away from Wilson. He stayed in bed for the rest of his term, which ended on March 4, 1921.

Wilson's second wife, Edith, cared for Wilson after his stroke in 1919. She is often called the "secret president" because of the work she did behind the scenes while Wilson recuperated.

A WEAK LEAGUE OF NATIONS

The League of Nations was established in 1920 to prevent future wars. If one country in the League of Nations was attacked, the other nations in the League would come to its aid. The League of Nations was based in Geneva, Switzerland. President Wilson convinced the Allied nations to join. Later, Germany joined. The United States never joined because the Senate did not approve the treaty or the League.

The most powerful nations argued about the purpose of the League. Then, Germany, Italy, and Japan attacked other countries. The League was not powerful enough to stop them. World War II broke out. The League did not operate during the war. In 1945, it was replaced by the United Nations.

Wilson's Achievements and Legacy

Wilson played a great leadership role in World War I. However, he is known for many other achievements. He was the first president to take office with a list of laws that he wanted Congress to pass.

> "I cannot refrain from saying it: I am not one of those who have the least anxiety about the triumph of the principles I have stood for." *Woodrow Wilson*

He especially wanted the country to be free of powerful trusts. His idea about trusts was like that of the "trust-busting" president, Theodore Roosevelt. Under Wilson, the Federal Trade Commission was set up. The job of this commission was to be sure that there was fair competition in business. It protected consumers from fraud.

Wilson made lasting changes to the way that banks are run. The Federal Reserve System set up during Wilson's presidency today controls interest rates that banks charge on loans.

Wilson succeeded in lowering tariffs. However, lower tariffs cut the amount of money paid to the federal government. To make up for the lost money, Wilson set up a federal income tax. The 16th Amendment to the Constitution, ratified in 1913, allowed for this tax on earnings. Wilson also supported the 19th

Woodrow Wilson served as president from 1913 to 1921.

Amendment, giving women the right to vote. This amendment was ratified in August 1920.

Other achievements included the first child labor laws and the first subsidies to farmers. His greatest achievement, however, may have been his idea for a League of Nations. For founding this organization, he won the 1919 Nobel Peace Prize.

In the 1920 election, Republican candidate Warren Harding was clearly against all of Wilson's progressive policies. He won by a landslide, beating the Democratic presidential nominee James M. Cox.

After Wilson left office, he stayed in Washington, D.C. He was too sick to work. One of his last public acts was to ride in the funeral procession of President Harding, who died in August 1923. Wilson died on February 3, 1924, and was entombed in the Washington National Cathedral.

Historians rank Woodrow Wilson as one of the most important U.S. presidents. He had high ideals. As governor of New Jersey, he helped bring about social and political reforms in state government. As president, he led the United States into World War I. After the war, he worked to establish a plan to prevent future wars. He was disappointed when the Senate did agree with his plan.

During the 1920s, voters rejected Wilson's progressive ideas. They elected presidents who wanted high tariffs to protect business. They elected presidents and members of Congress who did not value Wilson's ideas for solving world problems. Wilson believed that world powers had to work together. Wilson's ideas are part of a concept called "internationalism." Many people in the United States did not want anything to do with other countries. This idea is called "isolationism."

The 1930s brought the Great Depression and the start of World War II. People began to value Wilson's ideas. His ideas about internationalism helped future presidents deal with foreign countries. His idea for a League of Nations led to the founding of the United Nations in 1945.

Woodrow Wilson is entombed in Washington National Cathedral.

Warren Harding's Early Years and Early Political Career

Warren Harding was born on November 2, 1865, on a farm near what is now the town of Blooming Grove, Ohio. He was the first of eight children born to George and Phoebe Dickerson Harding. It was hard to make a living by farming. George Harding became a doctor to support his large family.

Warren started learning about newspapers when he was a boy. He learned to set type on the *Caledonia Argus*, a local newspaper.

In high school, Harding edited the school paper.

Harding was not sure what he wanted to do with his life. He passed a test in 1882 that enabled him to teach school, but he found teaching difficult. He sold insurance for a while and then took a job on a newspaper in Marion, Ohio, called the *Marion Democratic Mirror*. The newspaper fired him in 1884 because he supported the Republican candidate for president. At that time, another newspaper was for sale. Harding and two friends bought the *Marion Star*. They struggled to keep the newspaper going.

Warren Harding worked for newspapers before becoming a politician.

Life changed greatly for Harding after he married Florence Kling De Wolfe. She was five years older than him and had been divorced. Florence had a 10-year-old son from her previous marriage, but Warren and Florence did not have any children together. Florence was a smart woman and wanted her husband to do well. She worked to make the *Marion Star* a successful newspaper. Ohio politicians liked Harding's newspaper. It was fair to both political parties and rarely printed negative stories.

Harding was friendly and a good public speaker. People began to think of him as a leader. Soon, Harding entered politics as a conservative Republican. He believed in leaving businesses alone and not imposing restrictions or regulations on them. Harding was elected an Ohio state senator in 1899.

Harding met Harry Daugherty, a political campaign manager. Daugherty helped Harding became lieutenant governor in 1903. He helped Harding run for governor in 1910, but Harding lost the election.

Soon, Harding became known to Republican leaders across the country. In 1912, they chose Harding to nominate William

Howard Taft at their convention. Harding was then chosen to be chairman of the 1916 Republican National Convention. In 1914, Harding ran for the U.S. Senate and was elected.

As a senator, Harding did not introduce any bills. He was often absent from Senate sessions. When he was there, he voted the way the Republican leaders wanted him to vote.

Harry Daugherty managed Harding's campaigns. Harding later appointed Daugherty as attorney general.

Harding's Presidency and Legacy

Daugherty urged Republicans to nominate Harding for president in 1920. The delegates could not agree on any of the other three candidates, so Republican leaders chose Harding.

Americans were tired of the sacrifices they made during World War I. They wanted life to be as it was before the war. Harding promised voters a "return to normalcy." Harding did not campaign by traveling from state to state making speeches. Instead, he gave speeches to visitors who came to see him at his home in Marion.

A large majority of voters elected Harding. Women voted in this election for the first time. It was the first time that election results were broadcast over radio.

President Harding showed little leadership. He let Congress and his Cabinet make important decisions. Harding appointed Daugherty as attorney general. Daugherty and some other cabinet members were more interested in making money than serving the country. The friends Harding brought into government were called the "Ohio gang." Soon, Harding learned that the friends he had trusted were doing illegal things. For example, the head of the veteran's bureau sold government medical supplies and kept the money. Later, Daugherty and others went on

The election of 1920 was the first time women were allowed to vote for president.

Warren Harding's administration was
full of corruption and scandal.

trial. Daugherty was never convicted,
but others went to prison.

To get away from the problems that his
friends were causing, Harding took a trip
to Alaska in 1923. On the way back to
Washington, D.C., Harding became ill.
He died on August 2, 1923.

Most people did not yet know
about all the wrongdoing in Harding's
administration. People were sad about his
death. They made speeches calling him
an "ideal American." After Harding's
death, Vice President Calvin Coolidge
was sworn in as president.

Historians say that Harding was one
of the worst presidents in U.S. history.
There were, however, some good things
accomplished while he was president.
A system for making one yearly
government budget was set up. Harding
supported helping farmers by giving
them credit to buy farm equipment
and livestock. Harding is best
remembered, however, for doing
nothing to stop his friends from
cheating the U.S. government.

"America's present need is not
heroics, but healing; not nostrums
but normalcy; not revolution, but
restoration…" *Warren Harding*

TEAPOT DOME SCANDAL

The worst **scandal** of the Harding
administration was the Teapot Dome
scandal. Secretary of the Interior Albert
B. Fall leased oil lands in Wyoming and
California to oil companies who wanted
to drill there. The companies gave him
about $300,000 in bribes for the land.
Fall tried to keep the deals secret by
claiming they involved national security.
When Congress investigated, Fall was
found guilty of crimes and was sent to
prison. The scandal was named for a
rock formation on the Wyoming land
that was owned by the government.

Calvin Coolidge's Early Years and Early Political Career

John Calvin and Victoria Josephine Coolidge celebrated Independence Day 1872, with the birth of a son. He was the first of two children. They named their son after his father, but they always called him Cal or Calvin. Calvin Coolidge later dropped his first name, John.

The Coolidge family lived in the village of Plymouth Notch, Vermont. Calvin's father owned a store and was involved in local politics. After a daughter was born, the family

"Prosperity is only an instrument to be used, not a deity to be worshiped."
Calvin Coolidge

bought a farm across from the store. Calvin helped with farm chores after his school lessons. His father taught him the importance of honesty and hard work. Calvin learned not to waste anything.

When Coolidge was 12 years old, his mother died. Five years later, his sister died. Coolidge was lonely. After high school, he enrolled in Amherst College, and he graduated in 1895. He then studied law in Northampton, Massachusetts.

In Northampton, Coolidge joined the Republican Party. His slow, steady rise as a political leader began. He served in just about every city and state political office possible, from being elected to the Northampton City Council in 1898 to being elected governor of Massachusetts in 1918. He became governor in 1919.

Calvin Coolidge was the 30th president of the United States.

Meanwhile, Coolidge met and married Grace Anna Goodhue, a teacher at a school for the hearing impaired. Coolidge was quiet and serious. Grace loved to laugh and have fun. According to one story, Coolidge brought home a bag of socks full of holes soon after they married. Grace asked him if he had married her just so she could mend his socks. Coolidge replied, "No, but I find it mighty handy."

In 1919, Governor Coolidge became nationally known because of a police strike in Boston. Without police to stop crime, mobs smashed windows and looted stores. Coolidge called out the state guard to stop the looters. When a labor union leader protested that the police had a right to strike, Coolidge replied, "There is no right to strike against the public safety by anybody, anywhere, any time." The people of Massachusetts liked Coolidge, and they re-elected him governor.

Governor Coolidge inspected troops brought in to regain control of Boston, Massachusetts, after the police strike in 1919.

Coolidge's Presidency and Legacy

The Republican Party chose Coolidge to run for vice president under Warren Harding in the 1920 election. Harding and Coolidge won. In 1923, Coolidge visited his father in Vermont. He was awakened soon after midnight on August 3 with the news that Harding was dead. Coolidge's father swore him in as president soon after, and Coolidge left for Washington, D.C., later that day.

In his presidency, Coolidge dealt with the scandals caused by Harding's friends. He appointed a commission to investigate. Coolidge let the investigators bring the guilty people to justice.

> **"... the chief business of the American people is business."**
> *Calvin Coolidge*

As president, Coolidge earned the nickname "Silent Cal." He was serious and said little. As a conservative, he continued the policies of Harding by supporting the needs of business. Coolidge passed several tax cuts for the wealthy. He favored high tariffs on imported goods and opposed U.S. membership in the League of Nations.

In the 1920s, many people thought they could get rich by "playing the stock market." They borrowed money to buy stock. Experts on the economy warned that this was dangerous and that an economic depression was coming. Meanwhile, prices for crops had fallen, and farmers advocated for farm relief bills so they could make their payments and keep their farms. Coolidge did nothing about the coming depression and vetoed farm relief bills.

Coolidge ran for election in 1924. His campaign slogan was "Keep Cool With Coolidge." During the campaign, Coolidge's youngest son died. Coolidge seemed to lose interest in being president, but he was elected. While on vacation in 1927, he handed reporters pieces of paper that said, "I do not choose to run for President in 1928."

Coolidge became president after the death of Warren Harding.

Herbert Hoover, another Republican, replaced Coolidge as president. Coolidge and his wife moved back to Northampton. They built an estate called The Beeches. In October 1929, less than a year after Coolidge left office, stock prices fell, and the stock market crashed. Some people lost all of their money. The stock market crash set off the Great Depression. At first, Coolidge thought he could have done more to prevent the depression. Later, he decided that there was nothing any president could have done. Coolidge died on January 5, 1933, and was buried in Plymouth Notch.

One of Coolidge's main accomplishments was to restore people's faith in government after the scandals of Harding's presidency. Some people blame Coolidge for the Great Depression, believing that he could have done more to help farmers and working-class people. Coolidge's tax cuts only benefitted the wealthy and led to the unfair distribution of wealth.

THE ROARING TWENTIES

The 1920s were a time of prosperity for many people. Everyone wanted to forget about the problems of World War I. People wanted to have a good time. They bought Ford's Model T automobiles. Young women called "flappers" wore short skirts and long strings of beads. The 1920s were also called "The Jazz Age." People danced to this jazz music. They jammed theaters to see Charlie Chaplin and other movie stars. In the Roaring Twenties, it seemed like the good times would never end. The good times came to a halt when the stock market crashed in 1929.

Crowds gathered on Wall Street in New York City after the stock market crash in 1929.

Timeline

The United States emerged as a modern nation from 1900 to 1930. At home, many progressive measures were passed to regulate businesses and protect workers and consumers. Abroad, the world recognized the United States as a world power that would defend itself and its neighbors and allies. The U.S. government modernized during this era. Many of the government departments that were

1880s	1890s	1900-1908
PRESIDENTS		
Roosevelt is elected to the New York state assembly. After his wife and mother die in 1884, Roosevelt leaves politics to become a rancher. 	In 1898, Roosevelt organizes the Rough Riders to fight in Cuba during the Spanish-American War.	As vice president, Roosevelt becomes president after McKinley is shot and killed in 1901. Roosevelt begins breaking up trusts and is elected to a second term in 1904.
UNITED STATES		
The Statue of Liberty was presented to the United States by the people of France in 1884 and dedicated in New York Harbor in 1886.	Ellis Island begins to receive immigrants to the United States in 1892. 	In 1904, U.S. engineers begin work on the Panama Canal.
WORLD		
In 1882, Italy, Germany, and Austria-Hungary sign the Triple Alliance, an agreement to defend one another if one of them is attacked.	Spain gives Puerto Rico, Guam, and the Philippines to the United States after losing the Spanish-American War in 1898. 	Queen Victoria of Great Britain dies in 1901. Her son, Edward VII, becomes king.

established during this time are still in place today. Americans sacrificed their time and their lives to protect U.S. interests in Europe and support the Allies in World War I. After the war, the United States looked forward to prosperous times. Many people made risky financial decisions that they would come to regret. The stock market crash of 1929 and the Great Depression were right around the corner.

1909-1912	1913-1920	1920s
PRESIDENTS		
Taft, Roosevelt's choice of successor, becomes president in 1909. He sides with conservative Republicans. 	Democrat Woodrow Wilson becomes president in 1913 and continues progressive reforms. In 1917, Wilson asks Congress to declare war on Germany.	Conservative Republican Calvin Coolidge becomes president in 1923 after Harding dies. Coolidge is elected to a full term in 1924. 
UNITED STATES		
In 1909, the National Association for the Advancement of Colored People was founded to prevent violence against African Americans.	The United States enters World War I in 1917. 	The United States experiences the "Roaring Twenties," a prosperous time for many Americans.
WORLD		
In 1912, the British ocean liner *Titanic* strikes an iceberg and sinks in the Atlantic Ocean. 	World War I begins in Europe in 1914.	In 1922, Mussolini becomes prime minister of Italy and sets up a Fascist government.

Activity

The election of presidents and other government officials is the most important event in a democracy. No one can stay in office if the voters do not want him or her.

In the United States, every elected official serves for a set amount of time. This time is call a term. In the United States, presidents and vice presidents serve a four-year term. Every four years, voters go to places called polls and cast ballots for the people they believe will make the best leaders.

Before a presidential election, political parties nominate, or select, a candidate for president. The process of choosing a party's candidate for president begins with smaller elections called primaries. In a primary, voters in a state select a candidate. Delegates for the candidate then go to a political party's national convention. The delegates select the party's candidate. For example, delegates to the Democratic National Convention choose the Democratic candidate. Delegates to the Republican National Convention choose the Republican candidate. The person nominated for president by the delegates then chooses a vice presidential candidate.

Each party's candidates campaign. They make speeches and run ads that tell what they would do if elected. In November of an election year, voters cast ballots for the candidates they like best.

Elections of presidents and vice presidents are indirect elections. The candidates are not elected directly by the voters. People called "electors" choose the president and vice president. Each state has a number of electors equal to the number of its senators and representatives. The electors vote for the candidate who gets the most votes in that state.

Think about when the next election for president will be held in the United States. What events are taking place in the country. What would you do if you were elected president?

Imagine that you have been nominated for president. Make a list of the problems that you think you can solve as president. Write down the promises that you would make to the voters. Make a list of the leadership characteristics a president should have. Use the lists to write a campaign speech.

Quiz

1. True or False? Theodore Roosevelt had scarlet fever.

2. What nickname did President Theodore Roosevelt earn for breaking up monopolies?
   A. Big Stick
   B. Teddy Bear
   C. Trust-buster

3. Who became chief justice of the Supreme Court after serving as president?
   A. William Taft
   B. Theodore Roosevelt
   C. Woodrow Wilson

4. True or False? William Taft became president when Warren Harding died.

5. True or False? World War I began in 1914.

6. What was the nickname of the Progressive Party?
   A. Teddy Bear Party
   B. Conservative Republican Party
   C. Bull Moose Party

7. True or False? When the United States entered World War I, it was on the side of the Central Powers.

8. True or False? Republican President Roosevelt and Democratic President Wilson both believed in progressive social and political reforms.

9. Which two Modern Era presidents won Nobel Peace Prizes?
   A. Warren Harding and Calvin Coolidge
   B. William Taft and Warren Harding
   C. Theodore Roosevelt and Woodrow Wilson

Answers 1. False 2. C 3. A 4. False. Calvin Coolidge became president when Warren Harding died. 5. True 6. C 7. False. The United States entered World War I on the side of the Allies. 8. True 9. C

Further Research

Books

To find out more about United States presidents, visit your local library. Most libraries have computers that connect to a database for researching information. If you input a key word, you will be provided with a list of books in the library that contain information on that topic. Non-fiction books are arranged numerically, using their call number. Fiction books are organized alphabetically by the author's last name.

Websites

The World Wide Web is a good source of information. Reputable websites include government sites, educational sites, and online encyclopedias. Visit the following sites to learn more about U.S. presidents.

The official White House website offers a short history of the U.S. presidency, along with biographical sketches and portraits of all the presidents to date. **www.whitehouse.gov/history/presidents**

This website contains background information, election results, cabinet members, and notable events for each of the presidents. **www.ipl.org/div/potus**

Explore the lives and careers of every U.S. president on the PBS website. **www.pbs.org/wgbh/amex/presidents**

Glossary

armistice: an agreement to stop fighting

bribes: gives money or gifts for favors

conservatives: political leaders who believe in limited government, tradition, and stability, and want only gradual changes in society

convention: gathering of delegates to select a political party's candidates

corollary: a natural conclusion or result

corrupt: to change from good and lawful to bad and unlawful

delegates: people chosen as representatives

depression: a slow down in business that usually causes workers to lose jobs

dispute: an argument or disagreement

immigrants: people who come to live in a new country

progressives: political leaders who want to correct injustice in society through government action

rebates: the return of parts of a payment

reforms: puts an end to unfairness or wrongdoing

regulate: control with rules or laws

strike: refusal by workers to do a job until their demands are met

tariff: tax that a government charges on imported goods

trusts: monopolies, or control of industries by one company or individual

unions: groups of workers organized to demand better pay and working conditions

unsanitary: unclean and full of germs

Index